I0476431

Flawless Freelance Writing

How To Make A Fortune Freelance Writing

Brad Jones

Copyright © 2015 HRD Publishing

All rights reserved.

ISBN-13: 978-1515262442
ISBN-10: 1515262448

CONTENTS

INTRODUCTION

Are you thinking about getting into the freelance writing business?

It's certainly a wonderful new career option to think about and for many budding writers; they absolutely love what the industry has to offer. However, breaking into the freelance world isn't always simple especially when you first start out but it isn't impossible to succeed either.

This book gives you everything you need to know about how to get started in the freelance writing world and what directions you may consider taking too. If you want to leave your everyday job and choose a new path in life, freelance writing might just be for you.

You can learn about the legitimate websites to trust as well as the reputable ones to help get you started in writing too. No matter what your skill level may be, there will be a writing gig out there for you!

Don't delay, find out how to break into freelancing and become successful!

CAN ANYONE BREAK INTO WRITING AND MAKE A SERIOUS LIVING?

Can Anyone Write?

Absolutely! Anyone can become a successful freelance writer and ghostwriter as long as they have the passion to write. When someone has passion and the drive behind them, they can become a good writer. There are no special qualifications needed; only a keen eye and a skill for words; and for thousands of new writers, they start off with only a high school diploma behind them.

Writing is a talent learned over time, not in a classroom, despite what so many believe. It might seem important to have fancy qualifications behind you but actually, no, you don't need them in order to become a successful writer. Qualifications help in life but they won't necessarily make you a great writer; writers instead, need focus for their work and determination.

A writer's words come from within and no amount of qualifications will change that. Breaking into the freelance writing world doesn't require a degree and while this may open certain doors, it won't guarantee success, skill does. Skills make the writer.

Can You Start Anywhere?

Unless you get very lucky, almost every professional writer starts out at the bottom and works up the ladder. This is natural and it's how the process goes because you are inexperienced and very few clients are willing to pay big bucks for someone who's inexperienced.

Freelance writing is like every other industry, everyone begins their careers at the very bottom and no matter whether you want to write articles for a living or become a speech writer, you're starting place is firmly fixed to the bottom of the ladder. Of course, you might not like this idea but it isn't as bad as it sounds because once you start making a real living, you'll see the hard work paying off.

Can You Make A Serious Living Writing?

Initially, writing won't pay as much as other professions and it won't sound appealing especially when you get your first writing gig and it pays peanuts. Most lose faith here when they work twenty-four-seven and get little in return but actually, it can get rewarding when you stick to it.

There is no point in lying and saying you will earn thousands on your first writing gig because you won't unless you are very, very lucky and to be honest, that doesn't often happen. However, starting out is the toughest point because you struggle to break in and establish your name; but working long hours is a part of becoming a successful freelance writer.

There will be times when you work long hours and get paid little money and when this happens, you'll feel as though you will never make a living. However, you need to remember, you're just starting out and when you start out, it isn't all sunshine and roses, its hard work. If you're afraid of hard work, you're in the wrong line of business but if you like hard work; you are certainly in the right business.

It might sound a bit strange to say hard work is good but it can be because as you begin writing, you build a portfolio and establish your name in the freelancing world. You build on the bigger picture and as you undertake more writing projects, you gain experience and with experience, come more earning potential and soon you can make a steady living freelance writing.

Of course, you may not believe writing articles for little money is worth it, especially if you get less than $1 for 500 words but every piece of work you do builds an image of who you are. If the image is good, it opens the door to higher earnings and if you are a good writer, you can earn more in little time.

One significant difference between a good and a terrible writer, is confidence. Whenever someone has confidence, even a touch of confidence, it shines through in their work and gives a writer the credit they need to become a professional writer.

The World of Possibilities

In all honesty, there are now more doors open than ever before for freelance writers and ghostwriters. The simple answer – the internet – this must be where every writer starts in the modern world because it's a good avenue to find well paid writing jobs and get a foot on the ladder too. There is a bit of a hustle to get the best paying jobs but if you prove your worth, they can become yours. How bad do you want it?

The internet provides endless opportunities and possibilities for any professional writer breaking into the writing world. Of course, anyone can get into writing but soon, people can see who stands out above the rest of the crowd when writers establish their name. For those with no prior writing experience, the web is the best place to break into the industry.

Writers don't need to pay a penny to write, or rather shouldn't, and anyone who believes they need to is mistaken. The only thing you need to pay for is a good internet connection and a reliable computer! These are the only things writers need to invest money in, in order to start work.

Don't make the mistake of paying to work! Please! This can be valued advice for novice writers breaking into the industry.

Is Ghostwriting Impossible To Break Into?

Becoming a ghostwriter is in fact very simple to do and it's a really easy way to make extra cash and a good steady income. Ghostwriting is perfect for those who need flexibility and since you mostly work from home, you get the freedom you want. There are no 9-5 schedules because you actually create your own working hours and as long as you don't miss deadlines, you can earn thousands.

If you can create good relationships, the work can be endless and that is vital to becoming a successful freelancer. Making a living, a proper living from ghostwriting is quite simple and even if you aren't the most skilled person, you can quickly learn. That is why ghostwriting is very popular, and while the competition may be high, there is always someone looking for a skilled ghostwriter.

Never be afraid to write! Anyone can write and anyone can become a writer and make a serious living when they know how to break into the freelancing world.

Actions from This Chapter

- Understand Your Niche. Find out what topic you feel most capable writing; finance, marketing, and general informative articles, etc. If you're lacking in confidence or ideas, ask yourself "what are my passions in life?".

- Assess your writing skills. Understand your strengths and weaknesses. Are you more creative or factual based writer? Do you like including humor? Would your style suit Novels or Magazines?

- Test your skills by calculating how many words you can type per minute. (Employers can find this useful.)

- Understand what the normal rate per word is on the jobs you're interested in and set your prices competitively.

- Have a PayPal account set up (if you don't already) as some employers will choose to pay through this merchant.

- Set out a plan for the upcoming year. Say what you want to have achieved and access how far you have come over the next few months – Eg. Write an article a month? Write 3 books in 6 months? Or earn £1,000 this year?

EARNING MONEY WRITING – HOW AND WHERE SHOULD YOU START OUT?

Set Up a Free Email Account with Google

You may already have a personal email account set up but it can be important to create a second, separate email account just for work. Now, you may think there is no need but actually, you can easily overlook an important email from a client in an inbox filled with personal correspondence. This isn't the only reason to set up a separate email account but it's one of the best reasons to do so.

There are plenty of good and reliable email services to choose from including Google that offer free email accounts. If you were to choose Google, you can easily create a Google Mail (Gmail) account within a few minutes; and once the account is set up, you are free to receive emails. There is also a free 15 GB limit for the account so you can certainly store plenty of emails here before reaching the limit.

It will also be important to check the inbox regularly just in case a client wants to hire you. Missing just one email about work could cause a lot of problems; you might think you can easily get another writing gig but if you are not consistent with clients then it can go against your reputation online.

Prepare a Resume of Your Skills and a Sample Piece

A curriculum vitae or resume is important for anyone seeking employment. In most cases, the client wants to know what type of writer you are so it will be vital to have some sort of resume prepared for them. If you however, are choosing to not work online but rather apply to a company, they might want a full resume which includes work history, your experience and so forth. For those just starting out, applying to a writing company may not be the best course especially if you don't feel strong enough for a position as a ghostwriter for an international company.

If you are however applying to freelance writing gigs online, you want to have a short but precise resume highlighting your skills. The resume must list the real skills you have because clients and employers want to find people who are honest and trustworthy and lying about your skills is never a good idea. You can list almost anything but they need to be real skills and useful to the work at hand.

For example, if you were proficient in a second language, you should absolutely list that within the resume. Knowing a second language can be excellent for writers because it could lead to more high paying job opportunities and not just translation work. Even if you have a basic knowledge of a second language, list that but ensure you say it's basic. It shows good awareness and that you are willing to broaden your horizons too.

However, some clients may want to see previous samples of a writer's work. This can be an excellent platform to put forward a great showpiece and let potential employers know what you can do. If you haven't already got a sample piece written, take the time to do so because it can be a good stepping stone for future work.

Remember, to take your time on this piece and ensure its top quality too. It can help employers assess your abilities so don't be haphazard in your approach and don't try to be too over the top either. Short quality pieces work best.

Pay Per Article Websites

There are quite a few different but impressive Pay-Per-Article websites to choose from. These platforms offer newcomers the chance to see how the market works and dip their toes into the water. Most sites offer the chance for quick money in exchange for good articles and if you have the ability to write an article, you can earn money. The following are some great pay-per-article websites to consider.

HireWriters.Com

This website works very simply. Clients, who need articles written, submit their needs to the website and create job posts. The writers will then look through the posted listings and choose the article they want to write. Most writing posts are very straightforward to complete.

However, you need to sign up for a writer's account in order to start writing but this is a simple process. It takes minutes to create the account and everyone is accepted so you don't have to worry about submitting writing samples.

Since you start as a beginner, the jobs will generally pay the lowest amount, anything from $0.99 to $2.50 but the word count can range from 150 up to 500 so the range isn't terrible and its fair pay for those starting out.

However, as you earn positive feedback, you can move onto the level of 'General Writer'. You need three reviews with four stars or more in order to reach this level but the pay is more. There is also the 'Skilled Writer' level which earns more but again the feedback from clients needs to be really positive. The last level is 'Expert Writer' which can earn the highest; prices can range from $5 all the way up to $50 but be warned that prices can fluctuate depending on the clients need.

The higher rating status you earn, the more you get paid and it can be fairly good for someone just starting out. The amount of articles you can write is limitless so you can choose to write hundreds a day if you really wanted to. HireWriters.com is a good platform to get your feet wet but don't take on any assignment that you know you can't finish because bad feedback will bring a bad reputation.

Clients can at times ask for edits and some can be very choosy but in most cases, the clients are more than willing to pay for quality work. If the work is rejected it could be down to over-stuffing keywords so you need to be SEO wise. However, higher paying jobs are possible here.

Quality work could lead to more work being offered by the client too if they have additional projects. Clients can email your profile and ask if you would like to work on their articles which could create strong working relationships. In the beginning, HireWriters.com might not earn a huge a lot of money but it's a fairly good start and a good way to break into freelancing. Don't be put off by the amounts you earn in the beginning. Think of it as a long game. You need to work through this process to earn a lot of money in the future.

Be wary, clients won't pay for poor quality. Don't assume a lower paying job doesn't require quality writing. Make sure you give it everything you have, and that will increase you chance of larger paying jobs in the future. All of this work can become part of your portfolio when you're looking for those bigger jobs. EVERY JOB MATTERS!

Some jobs cover rewriting articles, and article which covers a variety of topics. Most are SEO orientated.

IWriter.com

IWriter.com is another great Pay-Per-Article website. The sign-up process is very simple; you fill out a few simple details and wait for the confirmation email to be sent through to your email account. Once the account becomes active, you are able to start accepting job posting.

However, like HireWriters.com, you start from the lowest level which is Standard. There is a fast track system to reach the highest level and start taking on the higher paying jobs but to be honest; there is no point in wasting extra cash. You will eventually reach the highest level and it's good to start at Standard because it allows you to get a taste of what the client's want.

After good feedback, you can move onto Premium Writer, then Elite and finally Elite Plus. The higher status you gain, the more money you can earn; the prices can range from $2.50 to $50 but the more seasoned writers on IWriter.com will earn more. Even a newcomer can reach Elite Plus status fairly quickly if they undertake more projects and do good work.

BREAK Studios

The application process for BREAK Studios can be a bit strict at times so newbie writers need to be a bit wary. Starting off here without taking on previous writing work may be risky however; it's still a good option for freelancers breaking into the industry. Writers need to fill out the application form online and wait for the company to approve the account; once it is, you are able to write content.

BREAK Studios will send out the article topic to you then you need to write and send the article over for approval. The quality needs to be fairly decent however because the company won't pay for poor quality. You absolutely need to produce your best work otherwise you're at risk of having work rejected and getting no pay.

For approved articles, payments will be made at the end of the month. However, precise monies for the articles vary from each assignment. BREAK Studios can actually be great for any newcomer as long as they are able to provide excellent content.

WiseGEEK

This is a fantastic outlet to consider especially for new writers. A lot of professionals look to WiseGEEK and it can pay fair amounts too. Articles generally pay between $10 and $14 which is actually good for anyone starting out; there aren't a huge amount of legit companies who will offer a high amount such as this.

When the articles are approved, the payments will be made via PayPal. A word of warning though, while the application process can be quite simple, this might not be an exceptionally fantastic idea for someone who really doesn't have any experience whatsoever. Writers with a little can find this is a good outlet but not for those with no writing experience ever.

Those who have done a little work in the freelancing world can find this is a good option to look at. However, if you are confident enough to believe your work is what the company is looking for, submit something and if you are rejected you can re-apply another time.

WiseGEEK have some speciality subjects so they may only be looking for certain people with insight into these areas.

Content and Revenue Sharing Sites

Revenue and content sharing sites are good for professional or serious writers but be warned, they are very hard work and they don't offer rewards quickly. Breaking into the freelance writing industry using the content and revenue sharing sites can be a good idea because they allow writers to build up a good portfolio online and it does help writers to get feedback from other writers too.

The following are some options to consider.

Hubpages

Hubpages is one content sharing website which can be really great for any writer because you can actually write about anything you want. You can offer recipes, reviews on movies, games – anything you can think about writing, you can submit.

Hubpages will review your first hub to check the quality, and once it's approved, it will go live online. Every article written and submitted to Hubpages will be checked for quality before it goes live anyway but over time, the articles can be checked again to ensure the quality is maintained. Poor quality articles don't usually last long but you get the chance to edit and make changes.

You can post a number of articles here and hope it earns money from fellow Hubpage users and followers. The more people who read your content, the more money you can earn but you have to ensure the standards are high.

Hubpages offer Amazon and EBay programs in which you can make money too – they are all quite impressive but they can take up a lot of work. These are not going to offer quick cash but if you are really willing to work at it, then submitting good quality articles to Hubpages, even one a day, can in time, offer some promising rewards.

Bukisa

Bukisa is actually a great content and revenue sharing site to consider. If you are using Hubpages, then you may also want to consider using this site too. Again, the money you will earn will build up over time, so if you are looking for quick cash, this isn't it. However, Bukisa can really help build your reputation and establish yourself as a writer.

New freelance writers choose to write on Bukisa as well as other platforms in order to make money and gain experience. Newcomers could take up some freelancing projects as well as write their own content for Bukisa too. It's a great way to actually start earning income over the upcoming months and remember, you will own the articles because they are your own content.

There are plenty of great content sharing websites in which you can earn passive income over a period of time, the above are just two of the more popular options to help give you an idea of what they are all about. Of course, content sharing is great for those who have the time and willingness to put in the effort. The earnings might seem small for new writers but if you stick to it, over time, they all add up and you can find it offers a lot of rewards.

Freelance Websites

Serious or professional freelance writers and ghostwriters always need to look for writing gigs that will bring in the cash so they can live day-to-day. Freelancing websites are really the best places to start because there are thousands of writing jobs available and it means you can start building your name.

For some, content sharing sites aren't for them because they don't have the patience or time to wait in order to make a living. They aren't for everyone and don't always guarantee income. However, freelancing sites offer a great way to get your feet on the ladder and earning money.

The following are a few trusted websites to consider using.

ODesk

oDesk is one of the biggest freelancing platforms available on the web. It is opened to any professional who wants to work and covers a variety of freelancing niches from graphic design to writing and translation. There are literally thousands of postings here so new writers should be able to find at least one type of job suitable for them.

oDesk is a fantastic platform to get into the writing world and the projects can be small, big or somewhere in-between. Clients can offer short one-off contracts of an ongoing, long-term contract if they so wish. The assignments range also but there is huge potential for finding long term and ongoing work too which is fantastic for newcomers breaking into the industry.

Clients can at times hire writers they've worked with before or even recommend them to others; even newcomers can get recommended for good work. Most clients are willing to pay for quality work and there are really lots of good paying jobs available.

There are however also lower paying jobs which can actually be good for newcomers. You might not want to choose the lower paying jobs but to be honest, its good practice for someone with little experience looking to build on it.

Remember, as writers gain more experience, it can lead to more work and better paid jobs too. Some clients seek out highly rated freelancers and can even recommend to others. You can get sought out by clients who are looking for serious and highly rated writers; and if you build a good portfolio here, it can lead to more possibilities.

Once you undertake an assignment and complete the work, you will be paid by the client. There is a small processing fee from oDesk when payment is sent but it's usually a dollar or two, nothing too outrageous.

For larger payments, more fees can be taken but it isn't excessive; it's really 10% of the final fee so it's acceptable.

You even get paid whenever and however you want; there is PayPal which arrives instantly or via Bank Transfer which can take anything up to a week to process. However, the waiting times aren't too long and in most cases, clients pay for quality work.

The earning potential is endless.

Guru.com

Guru.com is a fairly impressive website for freelancers but while it may be free to join, they do take a minor fee when you are accepted for a job. The fees can be anything from 3% to 7% which is quite steep but it can still be quite profitable for higher paying jobs. Beginners might be a little wary of these fees but in most cases, the fees aren't taken from your bank account but from the money received by the client.

It's very simple to create a profile and while you're creating it, you will get the chance to list your skills. You can list any skill really but you must remember to add only skills you have. Don't add things that are untrue.

Once the account is set up, you can search for job listings and apply for the ones you are interested in. If you are chosen, you complete the work and send off to the client and you get paid. You could end up working for someone on the other side of the world and still get paid fairly with Safe-Pay.

Freelancer.com

This is a fairly decent freelancing site and maybe one best for the beginners. There are tones of projects posted and lots of people looking for freelancers. However the payments can be lower for newbie projects. Some say this isn't as safe as other sites but thousands still use this and are paid.

Projects range from simple translation work to ongoing article writing. Some clients look for newcomers to start on a short-term contract and if they are good enough, add them to their writing teams for future work. Pay can be good at times too if you are able to get the better paying jobs. It isn't impossible, just a little harder but an OK site for newcomers breaking into the industry.

Freelancer.com takes a fee from every project awarded which isn't exactly great. There isn't however any fees to join up with a basic membership which is great but the amount of bids are reduced. You can increase the bids to bid on projects with different memberships but they can cost money. The basic account which is free is worth trying for newcomers to gain experience and earn a fair living.

Other Sources to Consider Starting Out

Blogging can also be a fantastic resource to consider when freelancing. This can offer some great cash and a great opportunity to make a serious living from home. However you must work at this long time in order to gain a good reputation and even make a good income. This can be hard work at times but if you put in a lot of work it can pay off.

Of course, blogging doesn't promise quick success but it can offer long term income for those who are able to put in the time. However for those who aren't sure about creating their own blog frequently look at guest-blogging. People pay good money for guest-blogging and it's a good way to earn a living too.

Submitting articles to newspapers and magazine is a good source but they can look for certain types of content. Reviewing sites are also good sources to consider but again you have to work at this to make decent money.

A WORD OF WARNING

If you choose to sign up to any pay-per-article or content sharing site, some may have certain geographical specifications so be wary to check this out. Also, some freelancing posting sites I've mentioned above such as oDesk are a lot safer to use than some others out there. Be wary of what sources you choose especially when you are starting out. I would suggest starting out with one of the many options above, which are tried and tested before trying something new.

Actions from This Chapter

- Choose and set up a free email account. (Google, Yahoo Mail, Zoho Mail, Outlook.com are just a few to consider, there are many more.)

- Research the websites you choose to submit work to as well as sites you choose to sign up to.

- Are sites are credible? Are you happy to use them?

WRITING JOBS YOU CAN EARN MONEY WITH IMMEDIATELY

You Have the Potential to Earn Thousands

Working as a freelance writer gives you the potential to make serious cash. You should know by now it won't make you millions of dollars however, when you establish a name and work hard, you'll find more job prospects and you can comfortably make thousands.

When a writer builds a name for themselves online, they have generally more work available to them. Remember, people seek good writers and you never know, one day you could be approached to be the ghostwriters of a biography for a politician or movie star looking to write their memoirs. It can happen but only if you're good enough.

As a freelance writer, you basically control what you earn because if you look for the work and put in the hours, you get paid fairly. However, if you're lazy and try to pass someone else's work as your own, it's likely to be your downfall. You need to make a living and you can, but it will take honesty and hard work.

Don't be fooled into believing you can trick a client; most people now use plagiarism tools to check the authenticity of a piece of writing. You may be clever but if you copy someone else's work then you won't be paid and you'll create a bad reputation.

Reputation Is Key

When you become a freelance ghostwriter, you instantly search for a gig; and when you complete the first assignment successfully, you achieve something very powerful. You get good feedback and believe me – that's worth gold. You don't have to be Shakespeare in order to be remembered.

From the very first ghostwriting assignment you take, you start to build your reputation and that will determine how much you make. Yes, there will be fussy clients out there who want things done a certain way but in all honesty, you have to put up with it because you are contracted to write what they want. If you can't complete something then don't say you can; getting in over your head is never a good sign and if you do, it might damage your reputation.

Even the smallest of ghostwriting assignments can say wonders about you as a writer. When you successfully complete a job, the client will give good feedback whether it's on a freelancing job posting site or anywhere else. Below, are some simple but fast ways to start earning money and build your reputation online.

Reviewer

Reviews are really very simple writing pieces; you may not technically be a ghostwriter but you are still writing and earning money. Self publishing authors are always on the lookout to give away a free copy of their book in order to get a review. Many pay people to post a very quick review online; it can be fairly decent money.

Basically, its five minutes of work but you can earn $5, maybe even more. This might not seem a huge amount and certainly not something you can make a living from but actually if you think about it, you can. Authors writing new books want and need people to leave good reviews of their book online and will pay for reviews which mean you can write dozens of minor reviews in the space of a few hours and earn a lot of money.

Many new freelancers find this is an easy way to step onto the ladder and it isn't too difficult either. If you can string a few coherent sentences together and share a positive view about the product, you can write a review. Right now, there are thousands of people looking for writers to post one review, even the worst typist can write a hundred-word review in five minutes.

When the reviews are good, the authors come back with another and another and soon you'll find the work piling up and the money waiting for you.

Short Blog Posts

New bloggers are always looking for fresh new content and willing to pay a pretty penny for it. Even if you don't own a blog, you can still earn a living from blogging. Thousands of bloggers need help creating content and offer writers the chance to earn anywhere from $10-50 on blog posts. Depending on the person hiring and length of content, the prices can vary but they can be quite profitable.

Shorter blog posts will bring in anything from $5 to $15 but remember that's per blog post. You could end up writing fifty one hundred word blog posts a day and earn hundreds doing so.

You don't even need to stick to just one client, as long as you can handle the work, you can take on several contracts at once!

Ad/Banner Writing

Banner and ad writing can vary considerably. Web owners are constantly looking for help to create new META tags and banner ads for their site. Most would rather contract the work out and that is where freelancers come into view. Any writer can take five minutes to write a small banner ad and earn $10. You could even write 10 ads in an hour meaning you could potentially earn $100 in just one hour.

Of course, different people pay different prices but if you can get a constant stream of work, then it can be very profitable for you. Banner ad work is very simple and thousands of businesses and corporations are looking for ad writers. It might not be fascinating work but it pays a lot of money.

Brochure/Newsletter Writing

Maybe newsletter and brochure writing doesn't sound the most appealing part of ghostwriting but actually it can pay well. Hotels, bars, restaurants, local and international companies are all looking for help to create good market content. Thousands of businesses send out brochures each year and need help creating these; if you can write snappy content and market a service then you have a good chance.

It's the same with newsletters. Businesses who are just going digital are looking for help to market their companies a bit more and look to newsletters to do so. The work can be fast and simple but very good paying. There have been projects for brochure writing of less than one thousand words that can pay almost $50-60. That's one example, if you are lucky enough to find these jobs, go ahead because they are well worth the money. In all honesty, you could complete a brochure within a few hours and it leaves more time for more.

Product Description and Content Writing

Content and product descriptions are very much the same because in a way, you are being paid to market a product. Product descriptions can be quick, pain-free and good paying gigs to consider. Getting a batch of fifty product descriptions with only a few hundred words each can be completed within a day or two and its excellent money too. Product description is fairly well paid gigs.

Content writing is quite varied. In most cases, the content will be for a website but it can also stretch to creating a home page, an 'about us' page; basically everything a website needs to go live. Content writing can be very well paid and it can be completed within a few days and then if the job is done right, you get paid well. Some website owners will offer fantastic prices for quality content; there have been people who offer well in excess of $300 for just a few pages for a website.

Its good money if you can get the assignments. What is more, these are relatively quick writing jobs that earn fast cash too.

Food Critic

Food critics don't all use blogs to do their talking, some still send their views off to newspapers and magazines. Some local newspapers or food-inspired magazines are on the lookout for good columnists and if you know a bit about food, it's a good option to consider. Magazines and newspapers pay different rates for different content but for one article you can earn decent money. Some magazines are willing to pay $50+ for just one article. Its good money especially if they want regular content.

Article Writing

Article writing can be a bit up and down. If you find good clients who are willing to pay for quality then you can earn anything and I do mean anything. The possibilities are endless but there are also some clients who will pay far less than $1 for 500-600 word content. This rate is fairly reasonable for those starting out, especially if you make a lot of mistakes. However, seasoned article writers should be earning more.

Some clients are willing to take the lowest contractors because they don't need to pay more but not all clients are like this. There are some fantastic clients who actually pay for high quality content and you can make decent money from this. Sometimes, you just have to sift through a few contractors to do so.

Travel Writing

To be honest, travel writing has become very popular over the years and it's not just with bloggers. If you have done travelling in the past, this might be the perfect niche for you. Even if you haven't travelled much but have a passion for it, this can be an excellent niche to concentrate on.

Travel agents and websites dedicated to travel and travel news are always looking for good travel writers. In a way, this is like reviewing and content writing because you can be asked to review a destination and you have to provide a lot of in-depth knowledge of local sights and tourist hot-spots but it can be profitable. Many travel writers earn between $10 and $100 per article. It isn't always the easiest of writing assignments but if you love travel, it's a potentially great idea.

Resume Writing

There are thousands of people across the world without a resume and struggle to create a stand-out resume. It's very tough but if you have even some basic experience with resume writing then this can be a very fast but effective way of earning a living. Most resume writers are able to finish the job within a day and as you gain more experience, within a few hours. You aren't rushing the work, it's quite simple to create a stand-out resume once you know how.

This can earn a writer an easy $50 for one resume and it could lead to long term work too.

Transcription, Editing and Proof-Reading

Thousands of novel writers and essay writers need to have their work corrected and are willing to pay a fair amount too. If you are good with a flare of picking up spelling and grammar errors, editing and proof-reading is the job for you. This can in fact earn you an easy $40-100 per short story or batch of articles. It can be fairly quick work too if you spot the mistakes quick enough. Proof-reading can be tiresome work but it's also a really good option for freelancers.

It's the same with transcription; if you are good at transcribing then this is a profitable option. You can transcribe audio or even old documents and put them into digital form, (such as Microsoft Word) but there is lots of transcription work out there. This can actually earn a lot of money, hundreds of dollars per assignment so it's a good way to earn a living.

Copywriting

Copywriting is an excellent way for a freelance writer to make a living writing today. It's perfect for those who love to promote something or just want to earn a decent wage. You can do anything from thinking up of catchy jingle lyrics to creating taglines for products, or slogans. It's endless and its one well paid writing jobs for freelancers.

Ghostwriting

The best thing about becoming a ghostwriter is that you can take on almost any assignment including novels, e-books and everything in-between! These jobs can vary because there is always someone out there looking for help to create a short story, a novel or even a few articles.

Ghostwriting can pay fairly well and once you have established a name or reputation within the writing industry, you can find you make a decent living too. Even though you don't personally get the credit, you make a good living! If you want recognition then sorry, ghostwriting isn't for you but this can pay well and it can range from a variety of non-fiction and fiction work.

Good ghostwriters earn a living because they put in the hours, put in the quality and their clients see that. Of course, the payments can range from the exact assignment but they are generally good paying jobs.

Screenwriting

You can be tasked to hire a manuscript for a movie, television show or radio which can pay really well. However, if you want to create your own script, it might not offer immediate results because the competition is fierce out there. For those who take screenwriting assignments, they can find they are great and fun. They pay well and many clients are willing to pay a minor portion of the final fee upfront, especially if it takes weeks.

Try and Test

If you are a complete and utter newcomer to the freelance writing world, you will feel a little out of your depth but don't panic. For most starting out, they can be a little confused as to which direction they should take but that is why you must try and test out different areas.

At first, you really want to stick simple but fairly well paid jobs in order to make a living. Take any assignment you see as long as you feel comfortable you can finish it to the best of your abilities. However, try out some review work, and then some article work and even some short story writing to see where your talents are best suited.

Have More Than One Niche

Let's face it, some freelancers and ghostwriters are going to have some idea of what type of writing they want to choose and that is fantastic but they may not always get the option of exclusively sticking to it. Having a niche, say, speech writing or ghostwriting novels is amazing because specializing in an area can always be useful but these jobs may not always be available to you.

In simple terms, you cannot sit around and wait for the next assignment to find you, you have to find it. At times, that will mean taking on other writing assignments like general article writing in order to make a comfortable living. Having a niche is great but you surely cannot just stick to one entirely; you need to make a real living and that sometimes, means taking projects you wouldn't normally take.

It's all a part of the freelancing experience.

Actions from This Chapter

- Try at least one job from the many options above. Can you earn money (regardless of the amount) in the next 7 days?

HOW TO GET REGULAR WORK WITH THE PERFECT PITCH

The Big Worries

Getting regular work when you're a freelance writer can be a big and often, a terrible worry especially when you have bills to pay. You must make a real living in order to survive but still many newcomers and even some seasoned writers struggle from time-to-time with getting regular work. Thousands believe freelance writers don't make enough money to live and while this may be true in some cases, writers can in fact earn good money and get regular work too. It's down to you!

It can be comforting to have constant well paid work bringing in the money to pay the bills however, there are actually thousands of freelancers who have a series of short and long contracts that pay their bills. Writers can make good money and make a serious living but you do have to know how to sell yourself. In all honesty, the pitch you offer will be the difference in getting regular work and no work.

Why Do You Need To Pitch Yourself To Employers?

Well, it's very simple; every writer needs to pitch their ideas whether they are hoping to land the job of writing a movie script or want to pitch the idea of an article. If you were to have the idea that you wanted to submit to a local magazine, you would need to pitch the idea you have to the editor. It's the same when you look for freelance work online; if you wanted to apply for a ghostwriting position, you would basically pitch your desire to take the role.

Employers don't just want to see someone's resume but also their pitch because it's this what tells someone a lot about you. Now, a pitch can be the difference between success and failure and for writers, it's their pitch which gets them regular work.

Most don't realize however, it's a vital tool in any writer's arsenal. A pitch tells an employer or client a lot about you. It's about being honest and respectful and your pitch could help build a bridge with the employer but how to write the perfect pitch?

Start With A Simple, Short Introduction

First and foremost, you must start with a brief introduction. This really should be short and precise because it's only introducing who you are. You don't want this to be long-winded, it should be right to the point.

Start off with your personal details such as your name, your skills and your niche of writing (ghostwriting, article writing, say what you specialize in). If you have any previously published work under your own name, say you're a published author also. It isn't always needed but always looks a bit more professional.

List Previous Writing Jobs You've Completed

Writers absolutely need to ensure their potential new employer knows a little about their past experiences. Employers want to know what they are getting with their new writer. You can list previous jobs such as guest-blogging or if you have your own blog, say so and give a brief list of project you've been involved with. Mention articles or books you've worked on before and try to include the jobs you think are most relevant to the role in which you're applying for now. Employers will want to see evidence of your writing ability. This bring me back to the point I made earlier – EVERY JOB MATTERS! If you've put the best efforts in with your previous jobs, no matter how small, it'll pay dividends in your pitch.

Discretely Do Some Name Dropping

Now, you shouldn't be too obvious when it comes to name dropping in your pitch because it might appear to be a bit big-headed. Instead, say you were asked by a certain employer to write a blog and name the blog also. The bigger the names, the more likely the employer is going to take notice. Of course, you don't always need to name drop especially if you don't have a huge amount of experience but it may help. Employers will have confidence in hiring you if other reputable people have done so.

Have a Respectful but Confident Tone

When you write your pitch, you absolutely must be honest, polite and very truthful. You may think about embellishing the words so that it enhances your chances of getting the job but if the employer finds you have been dishonest, you can forget regular work.

Be confident when writing and say things which are complimentary such as, 'I look forward to hear from you'. This is good but of course, you don't want to be too humble in your approach because it might make you sound a little desperate and that is never a good sign. Think respectful but confident.

Focus On What the Employer Needs

You don't want to ramble on and you certainly don't want to waffle on about subjects not relevant to the employer. Think about why the employer is posting a job and what he or she really needs. Is the person going away and need someone to cover from them full or part time; or does the person need a long-term contractor to work on their book or website?

These are the things you need to focus on because you have to apply to what they need. Employers probably don't want people who don't know what they are doing or don't appear to understand their needs either so ensure you focus on the job at hand and nothing else.

You must understand the project and what your responsibilities will be!

Offer Previous Work Samples

Before an employer asks to see samples of previous work, you should offer them first. You aren't trying to show off but rather showcase your talents and it also allows employers believe you aren't afraid and are genuine and authentic. Good freelance writers and ghostwriters aren't afraid to offer samples of their work and it's good to ensure employers know what type of writer you are. This creates confidence in the employer and if you're really convincing, they might not want to review it at all.

However, you shouldn't overload the employer with dozens of samples of work, one should be enough. You should only include the piece that is most relevant to the job you're applying to and remember, the sample allows the employer to get a measure of your abilities.

Let the Employer Know You Are the Writer for Them

When writing a pitch, you need to be forceful and let the employer know why they should choose to hire you. Let them know you are a competent writer and that you will always put your best work into their project. They want the best person to work on their project and not someone who is incompetent.

End With a Sincere Thank You

Ending a pitch can be a bit tough if it's something you aren't used to writing but it doesn't need to be difficult. You should wrap up the pitch nicely with a few simple words such as, 'I hope to hear from you soon', or 'thank you for taking the time to read my cover letter'. These are simple but effective ways to end a pitch.

Tips To Consider When Writing the Perfect Pitch

Writing a pitch can be very simple and if it's done correctly it can lead to constant, regular work. It's the perfect pitch that leads to regular work and believe me, it does because a good pitch reassures employers and shows how professional a writer is.

- Don't Let Things Run On For Too Long.

- Keep Points Short But Simple.

- Do Not Allow Your Train Of Thoughts To Wander Off.

- Remember, You Have Nothing To Lose By Applying To Different Jobs.

- Have A Positive Mindset

- Let Employers Know What Attracted You To Their Writing Gig.

- If At First You Don't Succeed, Try, Try, And Try Again!

Hopefully these little points will help you to create the perfect pitch.

Actions from This Chapter

- Write your first pitch and apply for a job.

- Create several pitches for different writing areas. Save them, and continually edit and improve them over time.

- **Don't stop trying**. Thomas Edison famously tried to create the incandescent light bulb 10,000 times before he achieved it. Keep trying and improving, and you'll eventually run out of failure options.

HOW CAN YOU BUILD YOUR REPUTATION IN THE WRITING INDUSTRY?

What Is Your Portfolio?

A writing portfolio houses a writer's past work such as novels, articles, blog posts, and everything else he or she has had a hand in. This is basically a real estate portfolio but instead of the properties a buyer has bought and sold, it shows writing pieces instead. However, most don't realize the importance of a portfolio and how it can make or break a reputation for a freelance writer.

Writers may start with a bare portfolio but as they build it, they also build their reputation. It's true, because every piece of writing allows a writer to create a reputation for themselves and their work. Like an investor, writers increase portfolios whenever they have a hand in creating a novel or an article.

It shows potential employers experience and what a writer has to offer.

It Takes Time to Build a Reputation

A reputation isn't built overnight, it takes real time so for any new freelancer looking to become an overnight sensation, think again. Unfortunately, success doesn't always come quickly especially in freelance writing; professional writers take time to build up a solid but professional reputation.

However, there are so many simple things to do to help build on a reputation in the writing industry. How can you build your reputation in the writing industry?

Join Writing Associations

If you have published any short stories or novels, you should think about joining a professional association. There are many great writing associations that showcase the work of published authors. This isn't always necessary if you haven't yet published anything but if you are, it's a good option to consider because it may help to build your reputation and of course, your portfolio.

Always Write High Quality Content

Writers who want to build their portfolios and reputations must write high quality content. It's that simple because quality is the biggest factor for a writer's reputation and whether you've been asked to write a small ad or a large novel, you absolutely must ensure its top quality. Quality work always brings a good reputation and it ensures people remember the name too and that goes a long, long way in building a strong reputation. Also, quality content does wonders for a portfolio too.

For example, if you were paid to write a novel, always do proper and thorough research. In fact, it's the same with any piece of writing; there always must be good research and an understanding of what you're writing about before writing it.

Think About Using Social Media

It seems everyone is on social media whether it's Facebook, Twitter, or LinkedIn and it could be useful for you. Some will use social media for keeping in contact with friends and family while others use it as a platform to build their online reputation. Social media could actually be a great method to use to help build a fairly impressive reputation.

Participate In Blogs and Forums Online

There are plenty of online forums and chat rooms that offer discussions on a variety of topics. These are some of the things you can get involved in but be wary of what you are commenting on. Sometimes, just adding comments on blogs can help build relationships with new friends and help boost your online presence. Of course, guest blogging will help to add more meat into the portfolio but don't just solely focus on blogging on other sites.

Create Your Own Blog

Everyone nowadays seems to be blogging about something and if you want to up your writing portfolio and build a good online reputation, blogging is the way to do so. This can be an excellent option for many new and upcoming writers and it is very easy to do. Of course, you still need to ensure your posts are good quality and useful for readers otherwise no-one will return.

Blogs need to be strong and if you constantly get viewers, then it will go towards building a strong reputation. This is what you want because there are now more and more bloggers coming to the forefront in the industry and are very talented too. There are more bloggers being widely recognized than ever before.

Create Professional Bios

If you have created any embarrassing webpage's or bios out there then it's about time to remove these. Sometimes, people won't take any writer serious if they are seen on their webpage in a very embarrassing pose because it doesn't look professional. Writers who want to build a good reputation needs to always remain professional; this doesn't mean you have to be boring but be wary of what you are posting online and that includes in bios and even on your own webpage too.

Instead, create professional looking bios so that if anyone should look for you before hiring, they can find a professional writer.

Think About Creating a Website

It might sound a little daunting creating your own website but actually it could be a great way to showcase your skills. Creating a website can help to build your internet reputation especially if the website is successful. Of course, you could simply have a website advertising your professional writing services with samples of your work there.

Some successful freelance writers and ghostwriters do this to advertise their work and earn a good living. It can help to build up your portfolio too and if the website is successful, it could be very promising.

Pitch Articles To National and Local Magazines and Sources

The internet is not the only place to create a good reputation and help beef up your portfolio. Many writers pitch ideas of articles or columns to newspapers and magazines and thousands get accepted each year. This could be the start of a completely new writing career but it could lead to long-term regular work and it means earning a good living too.

There are thousands of magazines out there from gardening, to cooking and big tabloid newspapers and they are always on the lookout for a new writer to contribute. If you can think of a newsworthy article, pitch the idea to different sources. This is another great way to get regular work in the writing industry and really boost your profile too because if you write a great article, newspapers and magazines may want you to contribute regularly.

Get Involved With the Local Community and Write a Community Newsletter

Writers who are active in the local community will find there are a lot of issues people have and what better way of getting those concerns to the attention of the right people than writing a newsletter? These can be perfect ways to help the community achieve what they want and at the same time, boost your profile.

Even if you don't always get involved with the community, find some pressing issues that are worrying local people and write about it. Create newsletters and you will see how much it goes towards improving and boosting your reputation as a writer.

Don't Make Mistakes Online With Social Media

To be honest, social media can be both your best friend and worst enemy especially when it comes to building a reputation. There have been many promising bloggers and writers who have made the mistake of posting something online in a tweet or post that comes back to bite them. Writers have the misfortune of writing things and posting them online only for the words to damage their careers.

That is why your personal thoughts about anything should stay personal. Writing things online can be good to express your thoughts but in terms of building a writer's reputation, it could seriously damage it! Think wisely before writing anything on social media.

Actions from This Chapter

- Get in touch with Social Media. Sign up to Facebook, Twitter and LinkedIn if you haven't already.

- Work towards getting at least 5 pieces of writing to put in your portfolio.

KEEPING THE CLIENT HAPPY WITHOUT BREAKING THE BANK

Why Do You Need To Keep The Client Happy?

Writers write and their sole purpose is to write quality content. When writers create good content, whether it's in article form or a story, it keeps people interested. Usually, quality writers get regular work and earn a decent living but only if they can offer excellent content. This isn't as difficult as it seems not if you put in the hard work.

However, when writers don't take care of their work, they usually deliver poor content and that leads to no returning work. Keeping the client happy is a must especially when it comes to becoming successful and getting regular work too. Remember, a happy client usually offers returning and often long-term work and that is the key for success but how can you keep your client happy and get regular work?

Be Honest In Your Application

When applying for a writing position, it's only right for a writer to be honest in every possible way. Clients are happy with honest and trustworthy writers but if someone lies and the clients find out about them, it spells trouble. If you lie in your application and the client finds out about it, you probably won't get any returning work and may even get a bad reputation too.

To be honest, there are writers who don't have experience in writing certain things but lie in order to get the job. The reason why they do this is simply because they think it will land them the job and it'll allow them to look more positively in the clients' eye. In reality, it's a big risk to take and once a client finds out they've been lied to, they probably won't want to continue working with you.

Respond To Job Offers Quickly

Check email inboxes regularly because clients hate being left waiting around, especially when their project hasn't even gotten off the ground! If you're late in replying or delay responding to them while waiting for something better to arrive, you're in big trouble. You may even lose the contract.

Late responses are a sign of bad manners and lack professionalism. That's why quick responses are vital. You must look at your inbox at scheduled points throughout the day and ensure no emails are missed as it can cost you work.

Don't Delay In Starting the Assignment

The worst possible thing a writer can do, is to say they will start the work on one day, only not to start until the day before the deadline. In most cases, the writer is rushed and it means the work is rushed too. Rushed work usually equals poor quality and that will result in an unhappy client.

As soon as you accept a job offer and receive the instructions, start. It's crazy to leave things to the last minute and honestly, the sooner you start, the sooner you will finish. The work won't be done any quicker until you actually start so don't delay in writing unless there is a genuine excuse to wait an extra day or two. The start is usually the hardest part. Once you take the step to start writing you can get into a rhythm. Just Start!

Have Clear Communications throughout the Contract

Writers can often start a project only to find they are a little unsure about something half-way through but many don't actually contact the client. This is a crazy thing to do because it could cause delays in getting paid especially if the client isn't happy.

However, when you have clear communications from start to finish, it allows both the client and writer to talk to one another. This will reduce the risk of writers making errors and if there is anything anyone is unsure of, they can clearly communicate their concerns with the other.

Communication is important for a writer and it's annoying not to get a response after emailing a writer for an update.

Clients aren't happy if they can't get in contact with their writers and if there is no clear communication, mistakes can be made.

Meet Your Deadlines Always

Writers who are able to make deadlines are always seen in a positive light – as long as the quality is good. Clients are always happy when their projects arrive before the deadline because let's face it, no one likes waiting for anything and clients can be very annoyed when left waiting.

That is why every writer absolutely needs to ensure they get the work done and to the client quickly. Going past deadlines shows less professionalism and generally reflects badly on the reputation of a writer too. A happy client loves writers who are able to finish the work before the deadline.

Make Changes That Are Requested

Sometimes, clients aren't happy with the finished product but it doesn't instantly mean they dislike the writer, it just means, they want to make some edits. Writers will understand this because work requires some edits from time-to-time so when the client requests changes, you must take it on the chin. You can't take edits personally because at the end of the day, you are the writer and you have been paid to write what the client wants.

If there are any requested edits, get to them quickly and ensure the client is happy. Don't argue about what needs changing. When you make the edits and send to the client, say you are happy to make any further changes. Its good practice and it shows your willingness to co-operate also.

Have you ever had your hair cut, and asked for changes to be made? Most of us have. Why? We're a paying customer and we want it to look a certain way. That doesn't make us or the barber right or wrong, it's about fulfilling the needs of the customer.

How do you feel when you ask the barber to change what they've done? For some of us it's easy, but for a lot of people it can be uncomfortable because you don't want to hurt their feelings. When your client asks you to make changes to your written work, they are a paying customer and we should want them to be happy. They might have also felt awkward about asking you. Make life easier for them, don't take it personally. Make the changes they request and be pleasant and gracious about it. This will stand you apart from your fellow writers.

Keeping Clients Happy Will Offer Regular Work

Writers, new and experienced, will understand how important it is to keep their clients happy whether they are being contracted for one article or several. One good written piece could lead to another and then another, and eventually it could lead to long-term contracts. Most will find they're able to get regular work when they leave their clients happy.

Anyone can write but it takes an exceptional writer to keep their clients passed with their work. Happy clients offer regular or recurring work and that is the key to earning a successful living.

Unhappy Clients Means Losing Money in More than One Way

When a client is left unhappy with a writer's work, it will reflect negatively. One possibility is clients may simply refuse to pay for poorly written work; another option is bad feedback. Bad feedback creates doubt in future clients minds, and could stop future work. You aren't just losing your reputation, but you're also losing money.

Unhappy clients won't pay for poor quality and it happens all the time! You can leave a client unhappy who may just pay you and leave bad feedback but others may do both! It's bad for a writer and their reputation. That's why keeping a happy client is vital to future success. If you understand what the client wants and put in the work the client has asked for, they will be left pleased and you will continue to find work and progress.

I'm not sure if I've made this point already but EVERY JOB MATTERS!

Actions to Take

- Practice writing articles to see the quality of your work. Ask a friend or family member to grade your work out of 10. If it isn't 10 out of 10. What would they suggest doing to make it 10 out of 10?

- When you get your first job aim to complete it 10-25% quicker than you agreed without compromising on quality – a 7 Day Task finished in 5 days or a 14 day task finished in 10 days.

- Be honest with your client and don't take any project on you aren't comfortable with.

HOW TO TAKE YOUR WRITING INCOME TO THE NEXT LEVEL

Writers mostly start their careers working for very little money. It's unfortunately true and no matter how skilled you are, you'll always start off at the very bottom which brings in little cash. It can be very disheartening when you dream of starting this high paying career but earning good money isn't impossible, you just have to know how to move up the ladder.

The writing industry is vast and there are always new writers breaking through but no one will pay a newcomer thousands for one writing gig when they haven't proved themselves. It's as simple as that because with no reputation and no portfolio, employers believe it's a risk to hire inexperienced writers; even if they are highly skilled. Today it isn't so much qualifications people are looking for, but experienced and what a writer has achieved.

To be honest, building a reputation takes time and it does mean most writers make little when they first start. However, writers build and eventually they earn a lot more but it's just getting to that point where writers break through the minimum pay grade barrier.

Network Your Talents

Networking might not sound fun especially for those who don't play a big part in the social media world but it can work to your advantage. Social media has its up and downs but it can help market a writer's potential. Freelance writers can and really should consider marketing their talents on the web through social media.

Increasing income potential is never easy but when you market your talents and network with other writers and employers, it opens up a new door to success. Of course, there are no guarantees that being on

Facebook or Twitter will earn you any more income but it can help you market yourself as a writer. This can lead to a big job opportunity; you never really know what could happen.

The more opportunities you have at your disposal, the more chances you have to make a success of it.

You Must Be Serious About Writing Professionally

Thousands of people say they would love to write but there are only a small number of people who actually get serious about it. This might sound strange but it's very much true because serious writers will take any writing gig in order to make ends meet and will continue to work on their writing skills too. However, those who aren't as serious will say they are going to do this and going to do that and never really get around to it. That isn't a serious or professional writer. One of the biggest ways writers take their income to the next level, is to get serious and take action.

Professional writers take their work serious and set their schedules to ensure each project they undertake is completed before time and in good quality too. A 'work whenever' attitude isn't the mark of a professional and no professionalism will lead to low paid work. Serious writers will often find themselves looking for work at every corner and loving what they do, even if they are writing about things they barely know or understand.

You want to increase productivity which means creating a schedule you can work to. You may want to have set hours, say 8 am to 4 am; and being especially organized when prioritizing work orders is vital to keeping the income flowing. Writers who have good schedules often get more work done and that can increase their income greatly too because employers see good work and often are willing to recommend for higher paying jobs.

Increase Your Rates

It's a dreaded time when writers raise their rates because many worry no-one will hire them if they increase their prices. However, that isn't exactly true because writers don't, or rather shouldn't continue to charge the same price forever. Things change, prices change and so does the quality which means, when you see changes, (more quality in your work) the prices should reflect that.

Writers can start off with charging $2.50 per 500 word article or blog posts because this is a pretty fair rate for newcomers and those gaining experience. However, this shouldn't be the price forever; writers can in fact raise the prices a little as their writing improves. It is however, a very bad idea to jump the prices up drastically.

For example, you can't go from a $2.50 article all the way up to $15 or $20 because no one will pay that unless, unless the article exceeds 1000-1500 words. Most clients are happy to pay for quality but at reasonable costs. Clients won't be fooled by someone they've previously worked with who charged them $2.50 for a 500 word article and six months later, are charging $15. If possible, rise to $5.00; this is still a good amount and even though it may not seem much of an increase, it's an increase and its all that matters! Any increase is a good increase!

Writers have to charge smart for their work and say someone asked a writer to create a 1000 word essay or article, the price should reflect the time it takes to research and write the piece. $15-20 is a fair price especially if it takes only an hour's work; most writers can write a 1000 word article within an hour and that's with research so asking for any more than $20 would be reaching.

Ghostwriting can considerably increase their earnings because they generally do a lot more work. For example, a short story with 1500 to 5000 words could be around $150, but they could charge less if they don't need to do much research and can finish within a day or two.

Writers should increase their rates but, and this is a big but, they still should remain flexible. Sometimes, clients want to hire writers because of their excellent work but can't quite afford their prices. However, remaining flexible with prices is great because it allows you to get work.

Jumping prices up 75 or 100% isn't always a good idea; sometimes, 20% is acceptable and helps to get more work. Remember, the increased rates may not seem a huge amount but it's an increase and any increase in income is fantastic. Clients are willing to pay for quality, so bare that in mind!

If you're at a stage where you're being offered work and you're unable to keep up with the volume demand. You're in a great position to charge more money. When there's an increase in quality and then demand, prices should increase!

Set Up a Website

A website might seem extreme hard work especially to gain high search engine rankings but it does wonders for writers looking to increase their income and expand more. This isn't so much of a business opportunity but a second way to boost your income because the site can help to bring in clients who want you to work for them.

However, you don't need to pay for anything when setting up a website because there are free web hosting services on offer and often you can register a free domain name too so there is no real need to pay a penny, especially when you're starting out. The only thing you need to worry about is getting it set up; and to be fair, you can take your time to set up the website to ensure its good quality. It's not a must-have for writers because most don't but it's certainly a good option when looking to increase income.

When you create the website, you want to think about having a section dedicated to showcasing articles you've personally written. Copyright and protect your work – which isn't difficult to do or costly – and have a selection of articles from a variety of topics. When readers search for articles online, they could find your website which could earn a little cash for your site but that isn't usually where to money comes from.

The second part of the website should be dedicated to offering writing services. There should be a page covering what writing services you offer – and only offer services you can deliver. The website should also have a section where potential customers can contact you to enquire about services.

However, a word of caution, before any work is done by yourself, there should be a contract between the client and yourself. Taking an upfront fee, say 5% is a good idea; others may disagree but it's always a good way to protect yourself from scammers who take the work and run.

Contribute To Magazines

One way to increase your income is to write with magazines. There are actually thousands of amazing magazines, including online magazines, which are constantly looking for new writers and contributors. Anyone can submit an interesting story or article to a magazine and if it's accepted you get paid. Magazines can pay anything from $20-100 per contribution so it can be excellent money for any writer. Of course, it's one great way to increase income but if an article isn't accepted by a magazine, try another. Remember Thomas Edison.

Magazines can often pay really well and there are so many of them out there that you can easily find one who will want to use your work. There are speciality magazines such as gardening, cooking and DIY, so if you are fairly knowledgeable about these topics, you have great potential to earn fairly decent income.

Look For More Well-Paying Work!

One great way to increase income would be to simply look for more work. This might seem the obvious answer but it's also the easiest one too. Writers who want to increase their income can increase the work load. However, that doesn't actually mean overloading the plate so much so you can't complete the work. Taking on additional work can supplement income and increase it too.

It would also be a great idea to start searching for better paying writing gigs. Increasing income can be rather simple when you continue to search for well-paid jobs and usually they aren't too difficult to find. If you are a great writer you can easily increase income by sticking with well-paid gigs. There is big competition out there but good writers can usually find the best paying work.

Diverse

Having a niche can be great for writers but it mightn't be the full driving force behind increasing your income. Writers who are able to offer only one niche can find the gigs available limited and that certainly means limited income and potential low pay. However, if you diverse your abilities and diverse your skills you can find more and sometimes, better paying gigs too.

It doesn't hurt to dip your feet into other areas of writing especially when it comes to increasing your income. Don't be afraid to look into other areas of writing because it can bring better money for you. Remember, you want to make a living so you really can't be choosy to begin with. If you're diverse, you'll be able to work in most writing areas and increase the chances for success. Having a niche is good and in time you might find something you're exceptional at. In the initial stages of freelance writing a broader approach is more likely to get you more work, experience and money.

For example, ghostwriting may be what you love and while these can be great paying jobs, you may not always find one of these gigs. If not, you could always try copywriting or article writing which always brings in fairly good money for expert writers.

Create a Business Plan with Goals

If you want to increase your writing income, which is effectively your business you must think about creating a business plan. You need to determine what the competition is out there and how you fit into it first and foremost. Secondly, you need to understand that you can't just stay at the level you are at now in order to earn good money.

Set out goals as to where you want to be, how much money you want to earn from writing and understand what type of writing you like most of all. If you want to focus on certain areas of writing, you need to look at the better paying jobs to help build a reputation.

Improve Your Writing Skills

As writers write, they continue to learn new things and when you're a professional writer, and want to boost income, you must first improve yourself. Any professional writer will tell you that because everyone starts with basic skills but as they continue to write, they broaden their minds and learn more.

Some writers start with just the ability to retell a story and nothing much else, while others start with very basic typing skills. Everyone is different but if you want to be successful in anything you do, you must seek continual improvement.

Firstly, it will be important to assess your writing abilities and weaknesses so you can see what exactly you're strongest at and what area needs the most work. Weaknesses can be turned into strengths in time, but without the knowledge, you won't know what or how to improve. Keep asking for feedback on all of your work.

Freelance writers looking to increase their income can often find it difficult to earn more but it's possible. Little improvements in your ability make a huge difference over time.

Making little changes including price changes and even broadening your niche can be worth it to help increase income.

Actions to Take

- Search and apply for higher paying jobs

- Get faster and be better - Improve your typing speed by practicing online. Can you increase your current words per minute count in the next month?

- Become the best you can be – Are there any local/online courses on writing you can take? Get a tutor or a writing coach to help work on your weaknesses and develop your strengths.

IS SELF PUBLISHING A GOOD AVENUE TO TRY?

What Is Self-Publishing?

Self-publishing is a brand new tool used for authors. Instead of using a professional publication house, writers can choose to independently publish on their own without a publisher. Privately printed work such as novels and e-books has become very popular and they are readily available to the public to purchase also.

Self-publishing can be hard work, more so than publishing the traditional way. Though, self-publishing is actually much simpler than having a publishing house accept a novel because publishing houses tend to be very particular in what they are looking for.

For self-publishing authors, they will have to do most of the bulk work themselves because they have to write the book then do the preparation themselves. That can mean more money (In preparing the book) and time. Only you will know if you're prepared to spend more time preparing the book for publishing. If you go it alone, you're likely to get more money in the long run, but you might need to have more money to begin with. Only you can decide if you think it's worth it.

How Risky Is This?

Authors who honestly believe they have an excellent e-book or novel but struggle to get it accepted by a publisher, can see the self-publishing route as a good option. They don't need to pitch their idea, they can just do the work themselves and get their book released. There are always risks involved with most things and it's no different with self-publishing. Professional publishers will carry vast amounts of experience, and that's hard to replicate that. Marketing a book is hard work and often difficult. A professional publisher will help a great deal in this area, but if authors put in the time, seek advice and learn, then it's possible to succeed on their own.

How To Self-Publish Your Work

After a writer completes a story and wants to self-publish, one of the first steps will be going through the work with a fine toothcomb. Successful ghostwriters and writers always ensure their work is top quality with no errors and mistakes. Editing your work cannot be understated here. You should proofread your work numerous times to ensure the writing is accurate. Can you get some help here? Ask a friend or family member to read it and look for mistakes. As they have a different perspective to you, they may find errors that you couldn't see.

After you've made all edits, it's time to find a self-publishing platform; this isn't too difficult because there are dozens of them. Amazon and CompletelyNovel.com are just a few, there are plenty of more impressive publishing platforms to use along with great self-publishing services. However, if you choose self-publishing houses or services, they can help do most of the work but they will charge for this.

Writers also need to create a title for their book as well as a memorable name. Most writers choose to use their own name but some use a pen name until their name in the writing world is established. However, the hardest part of going the self-publishing route must be how troublesome it is to actually market the book.

Marketing isn't easy and many new authors struggle to understand the importance of marketing correctly. Writers can choose to market the book themselves but some choose to hire professional marketers to publicize their book so more copies are sold and it's easily recognized.

You Can't afford To Publish Your Book And Publishers Aren't Interested, What now?

Ouch! It's still a possibility for some, but don't worry there is a way around it. You can self-publish your work into an E-book on an online format like Amazon. It's completely free to open a publishing account on Amazon (kdp.amazon.com). You'll need to get a design for the front cover of your book. You can easily find someone who can offer this service on oDesk and Fiverr for $5-$10. Once you have a cover, you can upload the writing, the E-book cover, and sell your book on Amazon for Kindle readers. You'll then receive royalties for every copy you sell.

This option will get your work out to readers, you can see first-hand how popular it is, and it's very cheap.

Always Keep Your Options Open

Self-publishing is a good option to take but it isn't for everyone. Traditional publishing is hard but it can be the better choice for those who don't know or want to get into the self-publishing world.

Can you afford a publisher? Do you have enough capital to publish a book yourself? Are you prepared to do the marketing?

It's important to keep your options open. Why not try selling your book on Amazon yourself and see if self-publishing is for you or not? If it isn't you can take your work to local publishers. If they won't publish it, ask for feedback as to why. Remember, the more options you have at your disposal, the more likely you are to succeed. Don't limit your options!

Actions from This Chapter

- Look closely at self-publishing costs. Can you afford it? Is this an option?

- Make sure you copyright your work before sending to any publisher or publishing house.

- Set up a publishing account on Amazon and self-publish at least one book.

- Contact at least 3 professional publishers and ask them if they would publish your book. (Remember Thomas Edison – he tried 9,999 times before succeeding)

DON'T MAKE THESE SIMPLE WRITING MISTAKES

Nasty errors can damage a writer's credibility, no doubt about that! Writers can and will make mistakes, crazy, stupid mistakes, but writers should also be able to catch them too. A good writer knows when they've made a mistake and you too must understand and pick up your mistakes quickly.

Grammatical errors are one of the easiest and damaging types of mistakes a writer can make. Even though they are easy to slip up with, a grammatical error can take the readers focus away from the writing, it can create doubt in the readers mind on your knowledge, and overall lower the value of your work.

There are dozens of simple errors to slip up on. The following are mistakes writers often make, hopefully you will learn from these and avoid them in the future.

Not Re-Reading the Work

Some writers actually write their first draft and send it off without ever looking it over. This can be a terrible thing to do because you can and probably will make mistakes. Most of the times, writers' minds wonder off in another direction and it leaves unnecessary sentences behind.

Writers absolutely need to take the time to look over what they have written. It doesn't matter whether it's a 100 word piece or 1000; it needs to be correct in every possible way including grammar and structure. Writers must be able to re-read and re-evaluate their own work in order to ensure there aren't any errors.

It doesn't take too long and it does reflect on a writer's reputation when they take extreme caution with their work too. Clients love to see perfection and love writers who have taken the time to actually re-read their work and stamp out errors too. Sending work off without looking it over could cost future work especially if there are lots of errors.

If you don't have the time or if you want to be extra vigilant, you can pay someone on a freelance website like oDesk or Fiverr to proofread it for you. I suggest that you edit it yourself, but at the very least, have someone do it for you.

Run-On Sentences

Writers can waffle at times in their work but it's important to be aware if you're one of them. Fortunately, professional writers know when to stop and you need to be the same. Yes, professionals run off with words but they also edit to shortened things to make it far easier to read and understand. Run-on sentences are terrible because they drone on for ages and are at times very unnecessary. This point re-empathizes the importance of editing. Proof read your work and question whether your sentences can be simplified or improved.

Adding Fluff Words To Up Word Count

One of the biggest mistakes writers can make is to buff their word counts by adding unnecessary words they don't need to. Fluffing words is ineffective and a common mistake some beginners make to get by. It looks unprofessional and it shows a lack of skill and quality. Clients hate when writers fluff words because it looks sloppy and they may feel that they've been taken advantage of. Do a thorough job for the client. It's better to go back to them with fewer words and ask for guidance, rather than pad out the word count.

Using Words You Don't Understand the Meaning Of

Every writer wants to look sophisticated, it's only natural but sometimes, it's best to stick with what you know. Writers often use big fancy words they don't understand and while it may make you look smarter on occasion, it can also make you look stupid if you pick the wrong word. Many new writers make the mistake of adding fancy words they don't understand and end up looking stupid. If in doubt, don't add something you don't understand. Look up the meaning or use another word.

57

Long Unbroken Paragraphs

It can be at times difficult to know when a new paragraph is needed but running one paragraph on for thirty lines is unnecessary. Lots of writers do have this bad habit and in all honesty, it's a mass of jumbled words and nothing more. It's difficult to digest for the reader. Make sure you break your work up into manageable chunks.

Using Inaccurate Information

One thing few writers spend the time doing, is checking their sources for accuracy. Now, you might not believe it's necessary to research everything you write but actually it's a very good idea. Thousands of writers make the mistake of using information which is simply untrue or incorrect and that makes them look incompetent. Use what you know or know what you use.

Talking About Something You Don't Understand

There is nothing worse than having a writer talk about something they don't simply understand. You must know what you are talking about in order to write about it but unfortunately some people don't!

If you are hired to write an essay on the English Civil War, you must research this and understand it. You don't necessarily need to know everything about the subject prior to writing about it, but you need to spend time researching it. It's the same principle with any article, novel, blog or ad; you need to write what you know about and if you don't know, educate yourself.

Changing Narrative Half Way through Writing

Starting off with 1st person view of writing before suddenly changing half way through to 3rd person view of writing isn't usually very effective. If you start with one style of writing, it makes sense to continue with that otherwise you could lose the audience.

You can change narrative in writing but only on special occasions. For example, if you were hired as a ghostwriter to write a crime novel, you can carefully view the points of both the criminal and detective's side. However, it needs to be well written and convincing; you can't simply have one page doing one thing and another, something completely different.

Actions for Chapter

- Look back over your work. Are you making any of these errors?

- Take action on each mistake you spot, and think about you can avoid doing the same thing in the future.

TOP TIPS FOR WRITERS TO SUCEED

Every writer has the potential to become a success and succeed in the writing industry. A lot of writers struggle to make it or take decades before really achieving what they want to. I've provided some tips that will increase your chances of success and speed up the process for you.

Top 5 Tips to Achieve Success

➤ Write As Much As Possible

➤ Set Achievable Goals You Want To Reach.

➤ Read As Much As You Can.

➤ Have A Notebook Ready For Ideas

➤ Use Writing Exercises

Observe Those around You

Being able to write naturally allows the words to flow freely on paper and there is nothing more natural than everyday people. Good writers sit and observe those around them and take inspiration from them; you can do the same. You could sit down in a park or even in a café and see how people interact with one another.

You can see how people talk and how they react with surrounding life. There is nothing worse than reading something a little too perfect because in real life that doesn't happen. It's the same with writing; things aren't perfect and that means using how people react in real life in your writing. Take the time to observe people and see how they actually act. You might find a story in something you see, or it might just ignite another idea you can write about.

Write Without Distraction

Any writer will tell you how difficult it is to concentrate on writing when there is music booming in the background and lots of noise going on around them. It's very distracting but that is why you must learn to shut the world out. You have to write without distraction it give it your all.

Have a place just for you – somewhere quiet and peaceful so you can write in peace. This can be important if you want to achieve anything in life and you will see a big difference when writing without distractions. If you don't have a spot like this currently, create one.

Get Support from a Writers Group

A writers group can be an excellent way to get feedback on short stories and your writing in general. The reason why is simply because you can bounce ideas from others in the same position as you as well as get real support from fellow writers. It doesn't matter if you want to write the next chart topping crime thriller or write articles for a living, writers groups are a great be around like-minded people. If you want to be successful in any field, you should spend time with people (preferably successful) who do the same thing. The higher the standard, the more you have to up your game to be around them. You can find an endless amount of local writers groups and a lot of them are free.

Proof-Read Carefully

This point has already been mentioned, but it has to be in this section because it's so important. All writers must proof-read all of their work. This is a must and so simple to do because when you take the time to read what you have written, you can start to see the areas that need improving. In fact, you can often be tempted to add more and make some edits.

Don't Be Afraid To Write

Too many people are afraid to try something and if you are too afraid to write then you aren't going to succeed. If you want to succeed in the writing world (or any world!), you can't be afraid of trying things out.

Question why you're afraid. Is it fear of rejection, do you not feel credible on the subject or do you worry what other people will think?

None of these reasons should stop you writing! If you really want to write, then don't let anything get in your way.

Write What You Know

The best tip for any writer is to simply write what you know. If you know about history, write about history, if you know about crime, write about crime. It's so simple. If you know a lot about something, it's usually because it's a hobby or a passion. Writing about a hobby or passion is usually much more enjoyable than writing about something you aren't interested in. It won't feel like a 'job', and you can enjoy the process. This will also increase the chances of you writing a better quality piece.

Actions from This Chapter

- Set up your own writing space

- Buy a notepad and carry it everywhere. You never know when you'll need it!

- Look online or in local newspapers for writing groups. Try it out for at least one week.

- Proofread all of your work at least 3 times!

DON'T DELAY, TAKE ACTION AND GET STARTED!

Just Get Started!

Procrastinating is is a common human trait. Writers in particular can suffer from this more than most, especially when it comes to writing the first paragraph. Saying you want to start freelance writing is great but you have to actually take steps to officially become one.

Who's to say what you have to write about, isn't important? When a writer continues to avoid doing something they find it is a lot harder to get started and write what they want. It's very much true and professional authors and freelancers will say the same thing.

Just write! Even if it's not the best quality at the time, it will allow you to get the words down on paper and get into a rhythm. Later, you'll be proofreading the work and you can change it then. Getting it down is the most important thing!

Starting with a blank screen is perfect because you have no distractions so, take the opportunity to write. It doesn't matter what you are writing about, start writing; it doesn't need to be perfect and it doesn't need to make sense initially. Don't worry about spelling mistakes, grammar or structure right now – just get the first draft down and completed.

Once the first draft is done, you've taken a great big step and now you need to re-draft it. For many, it's much easier to work through and adjust spelling or grammar mistakes than it is to creatively think about what you're trying to write.

Free Write

Free writing has become very popular for most people because it allows them to write down anything and everything. It's actually fun because you can write down ideas that you have as well as fill in any gaps or punch out a few ideas. Free writing is certainly going to help most freelancers get started because it allows them to get the feel of writing and gets their creative side flowing too.

Free writing is a prewriting technique in which a person writes continuously for a set period without any thought or regard to spelling, grammar or topic. It produces raw, often unusable material, but it helps a writer overcome blocks of procrastination, apathy and self criticism. Give it a try!

Force Yourself to Write

You don't necessarily need to write about the same thing each day as long as you continue to write. You could write anything as long as you write because if you don't write most days, that creativity will slowly slip away and if you love writing, you will want to write! However, sometimes, you need to force yourself to start and if it means forcing yourself to write, do what you have to. Try free writing to get yourself going again.

Set Goals

One great way to help freelancers break the cycle in the writing industry is to set out different goals. For example, writers can set out a set number of words they want to reach each day, say two thousand, and writers can work their way towards the goal. Goals help new writers get started especially when they begin to look for work. Writers can pen a piece of work they want to publish online or send to a publisher. It can give most people a sense of purpose to continue to write.

When you set your goals, try to make them specific and measurable (ie. 2,00o words), and have a time-scale (ie. Each day or in 6 hours).

I would also recommend finding your purpose for writing. Are you writing to make an extra $500 per month or for the relaxation it provides? Make a note of why you're doing it. The more emotion and power you can give to it, the more likely you'll keep going.

For example:

"I'm writing to provide me and my family with more money so we can pay off our credit card bills and go on two holidays a year. I want to write 2,000 words a day between Monday and Friday. I will earn $500 a month in 6 months time."

Actions to Take

- Try Free writing for 15-30 mins at least once.

- When NOW is the best time to write? Don't wait until tomorrow, write now right now!

RESOURCES TO CONSIDER USING

I want to share some of the resources I've found useful in freelance writing. There are many more options available online and locally to where you are, but hopefully a few of these will help get you started.

Mslexia.co.uk

Mslexia is an interesting little website to consider looking closely at. There is a great writing workshop perfect for those who want to write short stories; this can also be a valuable tool for any budding novelist too. However, there are blogs offering help in almost every aspect of writing and it's a good option for those who are a little lost too. Ghostwriters could be helped greatly here especially the short story workshop competition.

Best Writing Skills

This website contains a number of articles, 26 on the last count, which should help any new freelancer gain insight into common errors. There are articles containing tips for grammar, punctuation and everything in-between. There are also articles for ghostwriters who may struggle to write an entire feature length novel.

Copywriting 101: An Introduction to Copywriting

This website can be an excellent read for those looking to specifically get into the copywriting field. There is plenty of information about copywriting as well as how writers can understand their clients' needs and the market too. There is also help on how writers should go about getting noticed in copywriting circles.

Flash500.com

Flash500 is quite an interesting website because it doesn't have much information but has a huge list of fellow websites offering writers a good door into the business. The lists contain websites that run writing competitions, offer tips and everything else in-between including magazines who encourage writers to send their pieces into them. It may offer some good insight for writers who really want to up their earning potential and earn a higher income.

Freelancing Websites

Most freelance writers absolutely use different websites to find new job postings. They can be very useful and if you are serious about freelance writing, this may be an avenue you want to explore. Posting articles online may be what you're looking at but if you want to earn a good living, you may also want to look at freelancing websites to help build your portfolio and help make your name known also.

Actions from This Chapter

- Get to know what resources are out there. Use at least two of the suggestions above to get you started.

- Find another useful resource on your own that you would recommend.

OTHER BOOKS BY BRAD JONES

Ebay Excellence: Making Easy Money The Ebay Way

Fiverr Freedom: From Your First Gig To Making A Fortune On Fiverr

Blogging Brilliance: How To Make A Bundle On Your Blog

www.ingramcontent.com/pod-product-compliance
Lightning Source LLC
Chambersburg PA
CBHW070934180526
45168CB00003B/1073